Rookie
Read-About Science®

The Top and Bottom of the World

By Allan Fowler

Consultants

Linda Cornwell, Learning Resource Consultant,
Indiana Department of Education

Fay Robinson, Child Development Specialist

Lynne Kepler, Educational Consultant

℗ Children's Press®
A Division of Grolier Publishing
New York   London   Hong Kong   Sydney
Danbury, Connecticut

Project Editor: Downing Publishing Services
Designer: Herman Adler Design Group
Photo Researcher: Caroline Anderson

Library of Congress Cataloging-in-Publication Data

Fowler, Allan.
    The top and bottom of the world / by Allan Fowler.
      p. cm. – (Rookie read-about science)
    Includes index.
    Summary: Describes the location, climate, and animal life of the cold regions
at either end of the earth.
    ISBN 0-516-20321-5 (lib.bdg.)   0-516-26160-6 (pbk.)
    1. Polar regions—Juvenile literature. [l. Polar regions.] I. Title. II. Series
G590.F68   1997   96-28767
998–dc20   CIP
                                        AC

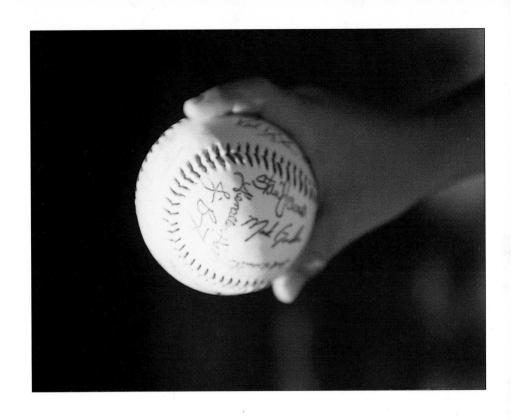

Try this. Hold a small
ball in one hand — with
one finger on the top and
your thumb at the bottom.

3

Now imagine your ball
is planet Earth.

Then each of these spots
would be one of Earth's
poles, the North Pole
or the South Pole.

The region around the
North Pole is called
the Arctic.

The region around the
South Pole is called
the Antarctic.

Both regions are always
very cold.

And both are "lands of
the midnight sun."

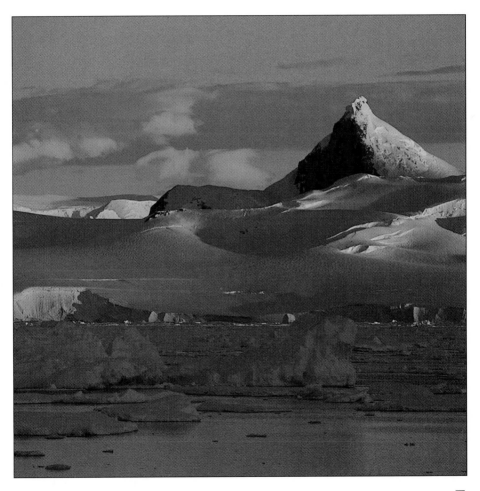

Summer lasts six months near the poles — and the sun can be seen in the sky all day and all night.

Winter lasts the other six months — and it's always dark.

You can't see the sun at all.

When it's summer at the
North Pole, it's winter at
the South Pole.

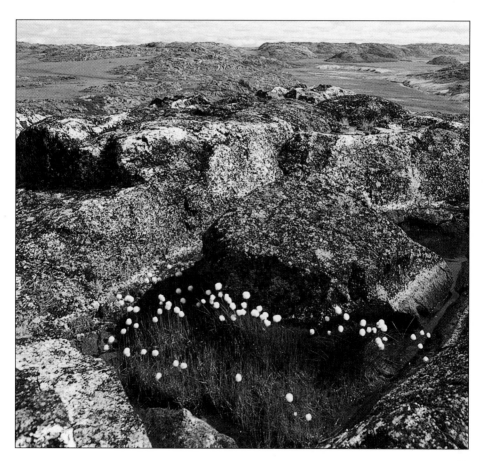

The North Pole is in the
middle of an ocean —
the Arctic Ocean.

The South Pole is in
the middle of land — a
mountainous continent
called Antarctica.

Much of the Arctic Ocean
is thick ice that never
melts. Nobody lives on
that ice.

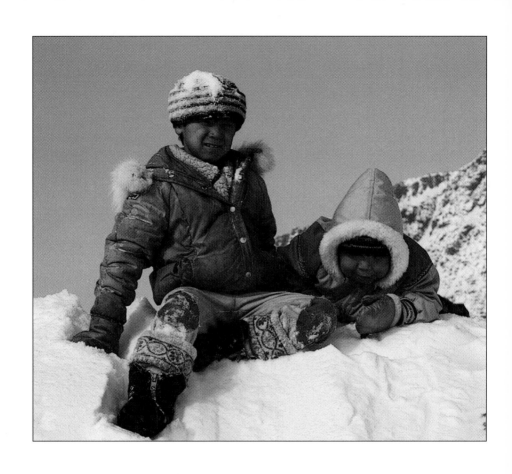

But a few hardy people live
in the cold lands touched
by the Arctic Ocean.

The Inuit of Canada and
Alaska sometimes make
houses out of blocks of hard
snow. These dome shaped
houses are called igloos.

The Laplanders of
northern Europe depend
on herds of reindeer for
food and clothing.

Heavy-coated animals such as Arctic hares, Arctic foxes, and polar bears live in the Arctic lands.

On the shores of Arctic islands, there are many colonies of puffins. These birds dive for fish, which they catch in their big, brightly colored beaks.

Whales, seals, and walruses
swim in Arctic waters.
Many of them visit
Antarctica in the summer,
along with some sea birds.

Beluga whales

Kerguelen fur seals

Walruses look much like
seals, except they are
larger and have tusks.

One bird, the Arctic
tern, nests and breeds
in the Arctic when it's
summer there.

Then, when winter
comes, the tern flies all the
way to Antarctica —
halfway around the world!

The only animals that live
all year long in Antarctica
are penguins and some
tiny insects.

And only a few simple
plants, such as mosses,
can grow there.

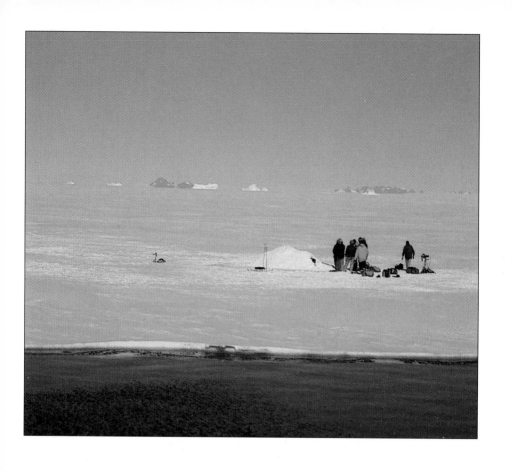

Scientists visit Antarctica to
study and explore it, but
no people live there.

Except for the mountains, almost all of Antarctica is covered by ice. The ice is as much as three miles thick.

Icebergs are big chunks of
Antarctic or Arctic ice that
break off and float away in
the ocean.

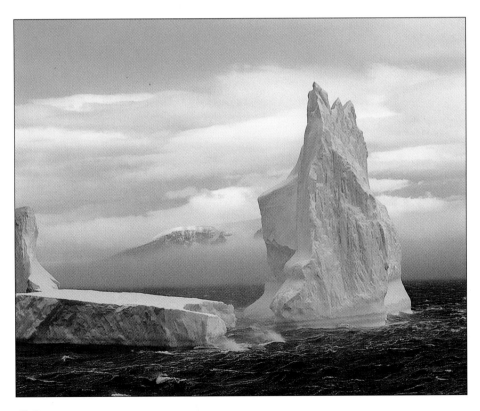

On a summer day in Antarctica, the temperature is likely to be about 0 degrees Fahrenheit.

On a winter day, it might be minus 70 degrees Fahrenheit.

Can you believe that Antarctica was once very warm, and full of vegetation?

Words You Know

North Pole (Arctic)

South Pole (Antarctic)

Inuits

Laplanders

icebergs

puffins

penguins

polar bears

whales

seals

Index

About the Author

Allan Fowler is a free-lance writer with a background in advertising.
Born in New York, he lives in Chicago now and enjoys traveling.

Photo Credits

©Wolfgang Kaehler — cover, 7, 13, 25, 26, 29, 30 (top right), 30 (bottom left), 31 (top left)

©Ben Klaffke — 3

Tony Stone Images, Inc. — ©Earth Imaging, 4

Valan Photos — ©Fred Bruemmer, 6, 14; ©John Eastcott/YVA Momatiuk, 9; ©Stephen J. Krasemann, 12, 18, 30 (top left), 31 (bottom left); ©Wayne Lankinen, 16, 31 (middle right); ©James M. Richards, 21; ©Joyce Photographics, 24

Alaska Stock Imaages — ©Chris Arend, 10; ©Johnny Johnson, 11, 19, 22, 31 (middle left), 31 (bottom right)

Photo Researchers, Inc. — ©Porterfield/Chickering, 15, 30 (bottom right); ©Stephen Dalton, 17, 31 (top right); ©George Holton/Ocelot, 23

COVER: Icebergs in the Antarctic Peninsula area